FAITH TO OVERCOME BROKENNESS

FAITH TO OVERCOME BROKENNESS

Bishop Oliver L. Jones Sr

XULON PRESS

Xulon Press
2301 Lucien Way #415
Maitland, FL 32751
407.339.4217
www.xulonpress.com

© 2022 by Bishop Oliver L. Jones Sr

Temple of Hope Church
9002 Parkway East C
Birmingham Al 35206

Paperback ISBN-13: 978-1-66286-548-0
Ebook ISBN-13: 978-1-66286-549-7

Table of Contents

Dedication

I would like to dedicate this book to my wife, Kennetta Jones, my children, and my church family, Temple of Hope. Also, to my siblings and to the memory of my father and mother, Mr. Oliver Jones and Mrs. Augusta Jones.

I love you all!

THE SEAL OF THE BISHOP OLIVER L. JONES SR.

PROVERBS 3:5-6

MARK 9:23

TEMPLE OF HOPE CHURCH
EPHESIANS 6:8 FELLOWSHIP

Acknowledgments

I want to thank all of those people who have challenged me to hang in there and not quit for their support on this project and your encouragement, which has helped me to write this book. It is my prayer that God's blessing be upon each of you, in Jesus's name!

Special thanks to my pastor, Dr. Michael D. Moore, and my mentor, Apostle IV Hilliard. Because of you speaking into my life and helping me to see that all was not lost, and that if I had faith and believed God, things would surely change for me and my family, I am a better man, pastor, and husband. Thank you both. Much love!

Introduction

For many years, people have asked me why I hadn't written a book about all of the things I had gone through. My response was that my story was just another sad tale of how life can go wrong for you even if you're living right, and I felt ashamed because I could not explain why things were going so bad for me. I even thought about taking my life a few times. I'm not saying I was perfect by any means. I just find myself talking to a lot of broken people in and out of the body of Christ, and many of them have asked me what I was waiting on. They shared with me how my testimony had been a blessing to their lives. My response is and always will be, to God be the glory.

So, after many years of praying about it, God has released me at this time to tell my story of how by His grace and through it all, I am still here doing His will and living life at a level I had only dreamed of. Though it has been hard, with a lot of ups and downs and much pain, my faith in God has brought me through. My hope for all who will read this book is that you will not give up and will hang on in faith until something happens. There is hope in Jesus Christ, and He will change your life forever. So, when you find yourself broken by life, remember that the God we serve still has all power, and He's able to bring you to the other side.

I have written this book in two parts. One talks about what happens when you're broken and includes my experiences, and the other is about what happens when the breakthrough comes. If you stay in faith, breakthrough will arrive, and you will be on your way to being a blessing to someone else. I believe that some things we go through in life are not just for us but the people who God allows us to come in contact with along life's path. I pray that you are blessed as you read.

> **Faith Requires Corresponding Action**

1

My Experience

Psalm 70:1

*Make haste, O God, to deliver me; make
haste to help me, O LORD.*

It's not easy to admit or talk about how life has broken
you over and over again, so as I share my story, it is my prayer
that the things I've experienced will help someone else overcome their brokenness. I was raised in a little town called
Flat Creek, Alabama. It was what you would call a mining
camp. Most of the men worked in the mines, and the women
did domestic work over the mountain. That's a country term,
meaning homemakers. Some of the women would also work
at restaurants. There was not a lot for children to do other
than go to church, so many of the activities centered around
this. We had daily chores like gathering coal and wood for
heat in the winter and feeding our livestock. And who could
forget general cleaning every Saturday morning? I guess you
can tell we lived in the country. Growing up as a child, I was

never really encouraged that things were going to get better. I tried playing sports like baseball, basketball, and football, and I would always get upset and lose my temper because I never wanted to lose. Rather than someone encouraging me to hang in there, everyone would laugh and talk about me. I don't think anyone realized how hard I was trying to just be accepted. I was hurting on the inside because I had been told I was never good enough. I remember how my grandfather would give my other siblings and cousins money for our school field trips, and whenever I would ask him for some, he would always say he didn't have anything; he never knew how that made me feel.

My daddy sang in a quartet and my mom in the choir. It wasn't long before I realized I had the gift as well. I started singing when I was five in the junior choir, but the people in our church were not in agreement with it because they had their rules, and according to them, I was not old enough. I had to be twelve, and their rules were more important to them than saving my life. After raising a little fuss, they let me in the choir, and I began singing more and more. It appeared that everyone was enjoying it, but no one knew or understood that something was happening to me. I was called to preach at twelve, but I couldn't tell anybody. You know if they didn't want me to sing, then preaching was out of the question, so I kept this to myself for a long time. I would go in the woods behind our house and preach what our pastor had preached that Sunday. Every time the church doors were open, I was there. I attended 22 revivals that year before I made my public announcement of my calling on AUG 17 1982. I was looking for something because of what I was feeling in my spirit. I could not explain what was going on, and it was hard keeping it from everyone, but I felt that no one would believe me. That night, I told my mother I had been called to preach.

Mark 6:4

But Jesus said unto them. A prophet is not without honour, but in his own country, and among his own kin, and his own house.

To this day, me being a preacher/pastor means nothing to some people. I know to some of them, I will never be anybody other than "Big-O" or Oliver. I have a lot of bad memories about my childhood, like the time I got a whipping for getting a plum off my grandmother's tree. Now, you don't understand—this was one of the worst beatings I had ever gotten. It was like my uncle was having too much fun doing it. Then there was the time that I was made to squat for hours until I was unable to stand without assistance. Growing up, I did not feel good about myself at all because I was told I would never be anything or have anyone. Life was very difficult for me as a child and teenager, having to lie about who I was and about what I was experiencing. When I was broken at one point in my life, I felt alone and abandoned, not knowing what to do or who to turn to. I made a lot of bad decisions and almost ruined my life. My uncle gave me my first drink at twelve. When I got old enough to buy alcohol, I drank every day. I've watched many of my relatives die from drinking, and now here I was, drinking all the time.

At this time, I was dealing with a lot of pain, and drinking helped me to cover it up—or so I thought. I would preach on Sunday morning, and as soon as church was over, on my way home, I would go in my trunk, and you know the rest. I tried smo king and also took my share of pills and many other things. It had become a big problem for me then. I was doing it more and more, just trying to belong. I received a lot of wrong advice as a young man. I was once told by a senior pastor that it was okay to drink, just don't let everybody know. I did not know that some of the people who I thought loved me actually wanted me to fail because it gave them something to talk about. I preached my first public sermon at eighteen from the Book of Job, chapters one and two, entitled "The Test." People were everywhere, and it was standing room only. I was thinking that all these people had come to praise God with me, only to find out many of them came to see my fall. I was told that day that I would not last as a preacher. It seems my whole life has been nothing but a test. Just when I thought things were about to turn around, I was told this by a pastor. I guess that was his way of helping me. Back then, the old pastors were judge and jury; they had the power to make you or break you. Real encouraging, wouldn't you say? I can't forget all the times I've been blackballed. The shameful part is that this kind of thing is still happening today. People were able to keep me from preaching in certain churches and having the opportunity to potentially become their pastor. I just wanted some help. When you're broken, nothing is certain, and there is no stability. Really, you will do just about anything to be accepted by those who mean so much to you, so you try everything to find a way out, only to make things worse. I went through a lot, never getting over one broken situation before another would occur. I began doubting myself, God, and everybody around me. I once heard a minister say that even doctors get sick and have to take the same medication they've prescribed for everybody else. I was telling everybody take God at His Word, that it will work for them; now it was my time to take my own advice.

Just a note: I've been preaching for forty-seven years and have been licensed and ordained for forty-one.

> **GOD IS**
> **FAITHFULL**

> **Stay In Faith Until
> Something
> Happens.**

2

When Breakthrough Comes

Psalm 121:1

I will lift up mine eyes unto the hills, from whence cometh my help.

To be broken means different things to different people. As for me, it was at that point in my life when I had tried everything I knew to make it, but nothing worked; people I had trusted were letting me down on every accord. I was living every day just going through the motions. Family called me the black sheep because of my skin color. I was being abused by family members, and my own brother stab me, telling me that no one would believe me. I told my mother about some of the things I experienced, and she cried and said, "Son, I didn't know." Church, I thought, was my only hope, only to find out that everybody in church is not saved. Some of the worst times of my life happened to me in church. Seeing one fight after another, wondering if this was what church was all about, it seemed that no one was hearing God. I thought I had seen it all, but then I became a pastor. Oh my God, it got much worse. I was accused of doing things like stealing or misusing money, running women, not preaching about what they wanted me to preach, and the list goes on. Law enforcement had to be called on two occasions. One was when I had gone out of town to preach, only to return home to a church meeting where the deacon had gotten together with a few members to vote me out. It got really bad, to the point that one of the ladies in the church brought her gun to church to keep me from preaching. On another occasion, the deacon decided to just tell me how he really felt. One Sunday, we were celebrating Christmas, and he walked up to me and said, "I could kill you." I have always been told that if someone tells you that, to believe it. Right after that, I resigned as pastor. I had to go court to face charges for trespassing. Of course, I wasn't guilty, but these brothers wanted me to suffer. They brought this charge to keep from honoring my contract, but after all of this, I did not want to preach anymore. I had had all I thought I could take. Feeling embarrassed and alone, with my heart broken, I was done. All of this for doing what I thought was right. Now I was wondering if it was worth it. I had told the church about a mortgage that was on the building that they were not aware of. This made some of the deacons very angry with me, so the crusade began to get rid of me, and I was like, *Here we go again.*

God Specializes In Putting Broken Lives Together.

Broken by life, family, and the saints, spiritually and fiscally, having gone through all of this, my heart was hurting, and I had no one to turn to. I tried everything I could to fix my life, only to make matters worse. I have met some mean people in my life, but I have learned through the Word of God that no matter what happened, I had to forgive them if I wanted God to forgive me. I have had some real troublesome times. It just looked like things were never going to get better, and all my hope was gone. Even now, there are people just like me who have no hope, and it feels like things are not going to turn around anytime soon. But I continued to preach Sunday after Sunday, not knowing what was going to happen next. I had to keep praying that something was going to happen real soon, that God would help me and see me through this bitter time in my life. Like the woman in Mark 5:25, she continued to look for help in spite of her condition getting worse. She made her way to Jesus, and I had to believe that a change was going to come for me too.

Mark 5:26
And had suffered many things of many physicians, and had spent all that she

had, and was nothing bettered, but rather grew worse.

You Can Overcome!

As I speak about these things, I am not blaming anyone. This was a real bitter time in my life when I wanted to quit. I was hurting, and no one understood me or what I was going through. I knew God had called me to preach, and I wanted to be a good preacher, but I had no idea of what I was about to go through. One bad experience after another, one bad relationship after another. It looked like everything was going wrong, and I couldn't do anything right. No matter how well people said I preached, it never felt like I did enough. I would cry every Sunday and ask God why I had to keep showing up week after week. I would talk to people who I thought were my friends, and they would say, "Jones, just preach the Word." Yes, I'm saying that preaching was not enough to make things better. It may have helped others, but not me. Let me add that at this time, I was not moving in faith. For real, I did not know anything about staying in faith for what I needed God to do. Like Abraham, I had to hold on to what I knew God had promised. I had to watch what I said about my own situation and learn real faith in a hurry, believing that better was possible.

Know that your faith in God can take you beyond human limitation.

Romans 4:20-21

[20]He staggered not at the promise of God through unbelief; but was strong in faith, giving glory to God. [21]And being fully persuaded that, what he had promised, he was able also to perform.

Abraham stayed in faith in spite of those around him doubting. He believed God that He would do just what He said. Abraham had three things working for him.

1. Confidence - He staggered not,
2. Consistency- He was strong in faith,
3. Conviction- He was fully persuaded.

It is your faith that makes the difference. I believe you see how important it is to stay in faith when you're broken. God will see you through.

The enemy comes after your confidence.

Psalm 69

[1] Save me, O God; for the waters are come in unto my soul. [2] I sink in deep mire,

11

where there is no standing: I am come into deep waters, where the floods overflow me. ³ I am weary of my crying: my throat is dried: mine eyes fail while I wait for my God. ⁴ They that hate me without a cause are more than the hairs of mine head: they that would destroy me, being mine enemies wrongfully are mighty: then I restored that which I took not away. ⁵ O God, thou knowest my foolishness; and my sins are not hid from thee. ⁶ Let not them that wait on thee, O Lord GOD of hosts, be ashamed for my sake: let not those that seek thee be confounded for my sake, O God of Israel. ⁷ Because for thy sake I have borne reproach; shame hath covered my face. ⁸ I am become a stranger unto my brethren, and an alien unto my mother's children. ⁹ For the zeal of thine house hath eaten me up; and the reproaches of them that reproached thee are fallen upon me. ¹⁰ When I wept, and chastened my soul with fasting, that was to my reproach. ¹¹ I made sackcloth also my garment; and I became a proverb to them.¹² They that sit in the gate speak against me; and I was the song of the drunkards.

I don't think enough people deal with their brokenness in this world. There are a lot of broken people in society, and you can see it by the decisions people make. People are desperate for help, and it shows by how present sin is. No one is asking God, "What must I do?" or "Where do I go from here?" Instead, they are looking for relief in all the wrong places and from all the wrong people. I was desperate for help or a way out and was holding all this stuff in. Being a pastor, I have heard it all, and it's always the same. People use sin as a way out and say they can't help it. They run to wherever they can find comfort for the moment, even though it's wrong. Let me be the one to tell you that sin is not the way. I committed my fair share of sin during this time in my life. You must turn back to God and repent of your wrongs, asking for His forgiveness, guidance, and grace, just as I did. The Bible says in **1 John 1:9,** "If we confess our sins, he is faithful and just to forgive us our sins and cleanse us from all unrighteousness."

John 3:7

Marvel not that I said unto thee, ye must be born again.

Acts 2:38

Then Peter said unto them, Repent, and be baptized every one of you in the name of Jesus Christ for the remission of sin, and ye shall receive the gift of the Holy Ghost.

I have spoken to my share of people who have experienced some type of brokenness in their lives. Some have felt alone and discouraged, while others have felt depressed. I would tell them that everything would be alright and to just turn to God, and He would take care of it. They would tell me, "Pastor, you don't understand what I'm going through." I couldn't tell them that I did understand because of how messed up I'd been in my life—been there, done that. I was taught in life to not let other people know you're weakness, but I believe that sometimes, the only way you're able to help others is by letting them know you've been through some stuff too. Now I tell everybody how my faith in God has changed my life and that I'll never be the same. I also think that if more of us who have gone through struggles would be transparent, we could help a lot more people to overcome their situations also.

Faith is seeing what Others Can't See.

> **Breakthrough cannot Come
> Without God on Your Side.**

> **You Can Experience Breakthrough!**

3

Broken But Not Beyond Repair

When the breakthrough comes:

1. REDEFINE THE MOMENT

He prays for deliverance.

Psalm 69

[13] But as for me, my prayer is unto thee, O LORD, in an acceptable time: O God, in the multitude of thy mercy here me, in the truth of thy salvation. [14] Deliver me out of the mire, and let me not sink: let me be delivered from them that hate me, and out of the deep waters. [15] Let not the waterflood overflow me, neither let the deep swallow me up, and let not the pit shut her mouth upon me. 16 Hear me, O LORD; for thy lovingkindness is good:

> *turn unto me according to the multitude
> of thy tender mercies. [17] And hide not thy
> face from thy servant; for I am in trouble:
> hear me speedily. [18] Draw nigh unto my
> soul, and redeem it: deliver me because
> of mine enemies. [19] Thou hast known my
> reproach, and my shame, and my dis-
> honour: mine adversaries are all before
> thee. [20] Reproach hath broken my heart;
> and I am full of heaviness: and I looked
> for some to take pity, but there was none;
> and for comforters, but I found none. [21]
> They gave me also gall for my meat; and
> in my thirst they gave me vinegar to drink.*

After many failures and bad decisions in life, I finally got a breakthrough. This is when things turn around for you and begin to work out in your favor, when you make up your mind to play the hand that life has dealt you and make the best of it—no more blaming everybody else for your problems. After praying time and time again for God's help year after year, God heard my prayer, and my life begin to change for the better. My break-through had come.

Take God at His Word.

In March 1999, the Lord gave me another chance to serve by allowing me to form the Temple of Hope Baptist Church with a few people who wanted a better life. They said to me, "Let's get it right this time, Pastor. We don't want to do the same things here that we did in the old church." So the work began. Yes, there have been challenges, but nothing like before—no fighting or false accusations, no assuming, just people working together to change lives for the kingdom to let men know there is still hope in Jesus Christ. In these twenty-three years, we have found out that we're better together. Make the best of whatever you find yourself in and make that moment work for you and not against you. We're working the plan that God has given us, and it is working for our good.

Romans 8:28

And we know that all things work together for good to them that love God, to them who are the called according to his purpose.

2. REDISCOVER WHO YOU ARE

Psalm 71

[1] In thee, O LORD, do I put my trust: let me never be put to confusion? [2] Deliver me in thy righteousness, and cause me

to escape: incline thine ear unto me, and save me. ³ Be thou my strong habitation, whereunto I may continually resort: thou hast given commandment to save me; for thou art my rock and my fortress. ⁴ Deliver me, O my God, out of the hand of the wicked, out of the hand of the unrighteous and cruel man. 5 For thou art my hope, O Lord GOD: thou art my trust from my youth. ⁶ By thee have I been holden up from the womb: thou art he that took me out of my mother's bowels: my praise shall be continually of thee. ⁷ I am as a wonder unto many; but thou art my strong refuge. ⁸ Let my mouth be filled with thy praise and with thy honour all the day. ⁹ Cast me not off in the time of old age; forsake me not when my strength faileth. ¹⁰ For mine enemies speak against me; and they that lay wait for my soul take counsel together, ¹¹ Saying, God hath forsaken him: persecute and take him; for there is none to deliver him. ¹² O God, be not far from me:

God is Faithful.

All my life, I was whatever anybody wanted me to be, but now, I am who God says I am. I am a child of the Most High God, a member of His kingdom. I am His servant, and I only need *His* acceptance or approval. I've had the privilege to travel across this country. I remember my very first flight in 1995 was to Los Angeles, California. I've had a couple of surface mentors in my life who have only spoken to whatever current situation I may have had going on but never to my soul. You see, I've tried a lot of things, I've seen a lot of things, and I've experienced a lot of things in my travels in the body of Christ that were so discouraging and disappointing, things I never wanted to be a part of. I saw all of these people who I looked up to drinking , smoking and a lot more and one day, it dawned on me that perhaps they were not happy either but just never had the courage to face it. For me, I tried doing some of these things that I saw them do, but I always got caught, never a happy ending. In reality, even with all the hats I wore as preacher, pastor, father, husband, son, brother, uncle, and friend, I was still broken. If you are going to overcome brokenness and enjoy breakthrough, you must discover who and whose you are. In 2003, my wife and I attended a church growth conference in Houston, Texas, and it was here that the pastor preached, "According to your faith, be it unto you." That word changed my life. I can't remember a time I felt like that. I think I cried every night in worship until I couldn't cry anymore. We went there looking for something, and boy, did we find it. This experience helped me to find myself.

No more mistaken identity or double roles. I can be myself, who God has made me to be. You must be comfortable with yourself and not try to be who or what you're not. A lot of people make this mistake. Know who you are in God and who He is to you. This is very important to your enjoyment of the next level of your life. We spend too much time trying to please other people when it really doesn't matter. The only thing that matters is that God is pleased with you. I wasted a lot of years and shed a lot of tears because I wasn't very confident in myself and needed the validation of others to feel good about myself. Well, I got myself together now. I know who I am in Christ, and I decided to trust Him no matter what or who comes or goes. He is my Lord, and I am His child. So, if you ever find yourself in a broken situation, find strength in your relationship with the Lord. Always be confident of who you are in Christ.

Psalms 46:1

God is our refuge and strength, a very present help in trouble.

3. REDEFINE YOUR RELATIONSHIP WITH GOD

Psalm 121

The great safety of the godly who put their trust in God's protection

A Song of degrees

[1] I will lift up mine eyes unto the hills, from whence cometh my help. [2] My help cometh from the LORD, which made heaven and earth. [3] He will not suffer thy foot to be moved: he that keepeth thee will not slumber. [4] Behold, he that keepeth Israel shall neither slumber nor sleep. [5] The LORD is thy keeper: the LORD is thy shade upon thy right hand. [6] The sun shall not smite thee by day, nor the moon by night. [7] The LORD shall preserve thee from all evil: he shall preserve thy soul. [8] The LORD shall preserve thy going out and thy coming in from this time forth, and even for evermore.

To overcome brokenness, you must have a good relationship with God. Oftentimes, when we are broken, our relationship with God can suffer. We don't think a lot about Him or what He is able to do or how He can handle all of our problems at the same time. When David was broken, he knew that God was his help. At that time when I was broken, I felt like God didn't care a whole lot about me, but He assured me that I belonged to Him, that He is my God and I am His child. Breakthrough cannot happen without God on your side.

Like David, I know where my help comes from, and He has promised never to leave me or forsake me. As long as I followed His instruction, I would have His protection. I feel now more than ever before that God is on my side and I am on the right track. Or as the old folks said, the right road. Now I fix it up with my Jesus, and everything is all right. I went through a time of doubting my call and everything by listening to people. I had to develop an ear for God. That was the word I received. Make sure you hear God, and in order to do this, you must have a relationship with Him.

4. RECONFIRM YOUR FAITH

Romans 10:17
So then faith cometh by hearing, and hearing by the word of God.

Mark 11:22-26
[22] And Jesus answering saith unto them, Have faith in God. [23] For verily I say unto you, That whosoever shall say unto this mountain, Be thou removed, and be thou

cast into the sea; and shall not doubt in his heart, but shall believe that those things which he saith shall come to pass; he shall have whatsoever he saith. [24] Therefore I say unto you, What things soever ye desire, when ye pray, believe that ye receive them, and ye shall have them. [25] And when ye stand praying, forgive, if ye have ought against any: that your Father also which is in heaven may forgive you're your trespasses. [26] But if ye do not forgive, neither will your Father which is in heaven forgive your trespasses.

This is so important in receiving your breakthrough. You must have faith that you are coming out and overcoming whatever has you broken. A few years ago, I was as low as I could go. When my dad died, I didn't care if I lived or died. I felt that the only person besides my grandmother who I mattered to was gone. I was still preaching, praying, and singing, but my faith was next to none.

Then my brother passed away, and my heart was hurting again. I loved him so much. He was younger than me, and for me to bury him? Wow, it was hard. I was broken myself but had to be strong for everybody else. I had preached my dad's homegoing service, but this was different. It hurt so bad. Here I was again, broken by another situation that I could do nothing about. Seeing him go through all of those treatments, I felt helpless. Then in 2016, another one of my brothers passed away, and in 2018, our daughter died in a car accident. The pain my wife and I felt was unexplainable. All we had to help us through was our faith in God. In 2020, my mother went home to be with the Lord, so let me tell you, I understand a little bit about pain and being broken—yes, the pastor, preacher, for more than forty years, was hurting and helpless. I talked to my pastor, who reminded me that I needed time to cry myself. Because the pain and hurt had been so real, I couldn't even tell anyone how I was feeling, not even my wife, so I cried every night and prayed, "Lord, help me please." I know that there are a lot of people out there who feel the same, like the man in Mark 9:24 whose son was sick and who carried him to Jesus and said to Him, "I believe but help thou my unbelief." Sometimes when you are hurting, you find yourself not in faith, but we must remember that God's Word is true, for in Numbers 23:19, "He is not a man that He should lie." After spending all my life preaching the Word and changing the lives of others, I can say that the Word has changed my life, and I'll never be the same.

He Keeps His Promises.

In overcoming my brokenness, my faith development has been one of the things I feel has been most important in handling all that I've faced in life. Studying the Word more, hearing the Word more, and speaking the Word more has made a difference in the way I see everything now. When I'm going through something now, I look to the Word to help me cope with life's challenges. I have learned that there are some things that happen in our lives that are not for us to deal with. We must learn to take our burdens to the Lord and leave them there. This revelation only comes when we develop our faith in God, so when I was dealing with all of my life problems and issues and the death of my loved ones, I knew I needed help that was not of this world. Thank God for His Word.

Faith Comes by Hearing.

I heard the Word of God preached, "According to your faith, be it unto you," and that I must believe and receive what I prayed for. Things began to happen for me that in all the years of preaching, I had never seen before. Next to having a relationship with God, this has to be the next most important factor in enjoying your break-through—developing your faith based on God's Word. I began confessing the Word every day over my life and my family, and we have seen God move time and time again, showing us His favor. I confess that the favor of God is on my life and new doors of opportunity are opening for me every day, that God desires for me to prosper, according to Isaiah 43:4 He has men for the vision and people for my life. I confess that He has men who will give unto me good measures; pressed down, shaken together, and running over will they give into my bosom. The only way to develop your faith is to spend time in the Word and change the way you think about things, believing that God will keep His promise. So, I say to you, when building your faith, you must watch what you say. Your mouth needs to be filled with faith words because it is a fruit tree, and the tree is known by its fruit.

At this point in my life, I desired to get my relationship with God in order. Only He could revive, restore, and recover my life. As I developed my faith from the teaching I received, I learned that I needed a plan to get my prayer life in order. I have been taught in life that you have to sow where you want to go, so I also started sowing like never before, believing God for change. Being in faith makes things happen. My bishop said that the promises of God are received by faith, and faith is manifested in what we say. Faith has to have an object; so I say to you, make God's Word and His Son, Jesus Christ, the object of your faith.

Romans 1:17

For therein is the righteousness of God revealed from faith to faith: as it is written, The just shall live by faith.

II Corinthians 5:7

(For we walk by faith, not by sight:) It is important that you be in faith when you're going through, for if you're in faith it assures God's help in.

5. DESIRE TO OBEY GOD

John 2:5

Whatever He saith unto you, do it.

I believe that if you obey God, you obligate God. I began to do what I knew God told me to in building the people of God, letting them know there's hope. God said to me, "Restore the hope of the hopeless, help the hurting, and bring healing to those who are broken." I stopped trying to please men and made God's will a priority in my life, allowing Him to redirect my relationships and the affairs of my life. I began to hang around with people I knew were living by faith and obeying God without a douzxbt.

Hebrews 6:12 says, *"Follow those who through faith and patient receive the promise."*

So, I started listening to the pastors who were teaching the Word without compromise. Now I hear the Word every day and make changes in my life based on the Word alone because I want all God has for me. God is a God of order, and to get all that He has for us, we must do things the way He wants them done. Here are a few scriptures that share the rewards available to us if we obey God.

Faith Comes by Hearing.

All throughout the Bible, there were those who through obedience received the promises of God.

Isaiah 1:19
If ye be willing and obedient, ye shall eat the good of the land:

Job 36:11
If they obey and serve him, they shall spend their days in prosperity, and their years in pleasures.

I Kings 17:15
And she went and did according to the saying of Elijah:

I Kings 17:16
And the barrel of meal wasted not, neither did the cruse of oil fail, according to the word of the LORD, which he spake by Elijah.

I began to look for those who I knew were doing what I desired to do. The first thing I did was pray for a spiritual covering. During most of this time, I belonged to a church, but I didn't have a pastor actively involved in my life. The Lord lead me to my pastor, Dr. Moore, who began giving me advice that would take me to levels in my life that I had never dreamed of, obeying God and stepping out of the box of tradition. This has brought a lot of criticism, but I am all about obeying God. As I said before, whatever He tells you to do, just do it. Your breakthrough depends on your willingness to have faith and obey Him. You must be willing to do whatever He tells you to do, for if you are broken, what do you have to lose? Take God at His Word. God is faithful, and He keeps His promises.

An Invitation To Salvation

This book has been inspired by my experiences in life and my relationship with God. It shares how things can go wrong, even if you are living right and going to church. Treat people with respect, and love everybody regardless of how they treat you. Know that good people go through these hardships too. Life can hurt you very badly, but take it from me—you can make it. Whatever you are facing, things really can turn around for you. Have faith in God because He has a plan for your life. Accept Jesus as Lord of your life today. He is able to bring you through your brokenness.

> **Faith is believing God over everything and everybody else.**

About Bishop Oliver L. Jones

Oliver L. Jones Sr. is the senior pastor of Temple of Hope Church, a Bible-teaching church located in Birmingham, Alabama. Bishop Jones has a passion for the heart and will of God. He travels extensively as a national evangelist and stands on his trusting in the Lord with all his heart. He is a man of great faith with a vision that changes lives.

Bishop Jones is the husband of Kennetta Jones and the father of Jessica,* LeDerrick, Oliver, Lauren, and Syraiya.

A Final Word

I pray that this book has been a blessing to you and that it will motivate you to hold on and not give up when you are going through life challenges.God will see you through. When He does it for you, be sure to help someone else.